ANIMALS
That Make a Difference!

Birds
새

Ashley Lee

Explore other books at:
WWW.ENGAGEBOOKS.COM

VANCOUVER, B.C.

ℯ→ WWW.ENGAGEBOOKS.COM

Birds: Level 1 Bilingual (English/Korean) (영어/한국어)
Animals That Make a Difference!
Lee, Ashley 1995 –
Text © 2021 Engage Books
Edited by: A.R. Roumanis
and Lauren Dick
Translated by: Gio Oh
Proofread by: Tamara Kazali

Text set in Arial Regular.
Chapter headings set in Arial Black.

FIRST EDITION / FIRST PRINTING

LIBRARY AND ARCHIVES CANADA CATALOGUING IN PUBLICATION

Title: Animals That Make a Difference: Birds Level 1 Bilingual (English/Korean) (영어/한국어)
Names: Lee, Ashley, author.

ISBN 978-1-77476-453-4 (hardcover)
ISBN 978-1-77476-452-7 (softcover)

Subjects:
LCSH: Birds—Juvenile literature
LCSH: Human-animal relationships—Juvenile literature

Classification: LCC RA644.C68 R682 2020 | DDC J614.5/92—DC23

Contents
목차

What Are Birds?
새는 무엇인가요?

Birds are animals with feathers and wings.

새는 깃털과 날개를 가진 동물이에요.

Most birds can fly.
대부분의 새들은 날 수 있어요.

What Do Birds Look Like?
새는 어떻게 생겼나요?

The smallest birds are bee hummingbirds. They are only 2.4 inches (6 centimeters) long. The largest birds are ostriches. They can be up to 9 feet (2.7 meters) tall.
가장 작은 새는 벌새에요. 벌새는 겨우 2.4인치(6센티미터)에요. 가장 큰 새는 타조에요. 타조는 9피트(2.7미터) 까지 자라요.

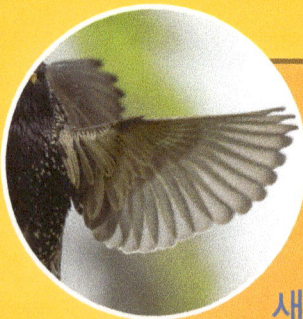

Birds have two wings. They are covered in feathers.
새는 날개가 두개 있어요. 깃털로 덮여 있지요.

Birds have a hard nose and mouth called a beak.
새는 부리라고 불리는 딱딱한 코와 입이 있어요.

Birds have sharp nails called claws.
새는 발톱이라고 불리는 손톱이 있어요.

Where Do Birds Live?
새는 어디서 사나요?

Birds live all over the world. They sleep in trees, logs, or under bushes.

새는 전 세계 모든 곳에서 살아요. 나무, 통나무 또는 수풀 밑에서 잠을 자요.

Kiwi birds are only found in New Zealand.
Ceylon magpies live in Sri Lanka. Madagascan
jacanas live on the coast of Madagascar.
키위 새는 뉴질랜드에서만 찾을 수 있어요. 까치는
스리랑카에 살아요. 마다가스카르자카나는
마다가스카르 해안에 살아요

Arctic
Ocean
북극해

Madagascar
마다가스카르

Europe
유럽

Asia
아시아

Sri Lanka
스리랑카

Pacific
Ocean
태평양

Africa
아프리카

Atlantic
Ocean
대서양

Australia
호주

New Zealand
뉴질랜드

2,000 miles
2,000 마일
0

0

4,000 kilometers
4,000 킬로미터

N

Legend 전설
Land 육지
Ocean 바다

9

What Do Birds Eat?
새는 무엇을 먹나요?

Birds eat many different foods. Some birds eat seeds, fruit, or insects.
새는 다양한 음식을 먹어요. 어떤 새들은 씨앗, 과일 또는 곤충을 먹어요.

Larger birds will eat fish or small animals. 큰 새들은 물고기나 작은 동물을 먹어요.

How Do Birds Talk to Each Other?
새는 서로 어떻게 이야기하나요?

Birds use special calls to find other birds, warn other birds of danger, or scare other animals away.

새는 다른 새들을 찾거나 위험을 경고하거나 다른 동물들을 겁주기 위해서 특별한 소리를 사용해요.

Some male birds do special dances to impress female birds.
몇몇 수컷 새들을 암컷 새들을 유혹하기 위해서 특별한 춤을 춰요.

Bird Life Cycle
새의 일생

Most female birds lay eggs in nests.
대부분 암컷 새들은 둥지에서 알을 낳아요.

They sit on their eggs to keep them warm.
그 위에 앉아서 알을 따뜻하게 해주기도 해요.

Most baby birds hatch after 10 to 21 days. They usually leave home after a few weeks.
새끼 새들은 10일에서 21일 이후에 부화해요. 그리고 몇주 뒤에 집을 떠납니다.

Some birds live longer than others. Most finches live for 5 to 10 years. The Laysan albatross can live for more than 60 years.
어떤 새들은 다른 새들보다 오래 살기도 해요. 되새류는 5년에서 10년을 살아요. 레이산알바트로스는 60년을 넘게 삽니다.

Curious Facts About Birds

Some birds fly to areas with warmer weather in the winter. This is called migration.
어떤 새들은 겨울에 따뜻한 지방으로 날아갑니다. 이것을 이주라고합니다.

Owls cannot move their eyes. Instead they can turn their heads in almost a complete circle.
올빼미는 눈을 못 움직입니다. 대신 올빼미는 완전한 원을 그리며 고개를 돌릴 수 있습니다.

Parrots and ravens can learn to talk.
앵무새와 까마귀는 말 하는 것을 배울 수 있습니다.

새에 대한 흥미로운 사실들

People once used pigeons to carry messages across long distances.
사람들은 한 때 편지를 멀리 전달하기 위해 비둘기를 사용했습니다.

Birds have hollow bones. They are filled with pockets of air.
새는 속이 빈 뼈를 가지고 있습니다. 공기 주머니로 차있습니다.

Over time, dinosaurs with feathers turned into birds.
시간이 지나면서 깃털이 있는 공룡들이 새로 진화했습니다.

17

Kinds of Birds
새의 종류

There are more than 10,000 different kinds of birds. All birds walk on two legs. Chickens are the most common kind of bird.

10,000개 이상 다른 종류의 새들이 있습니다. 모든 새들은 두다리로 걸어요. 닭이 가장 흔한 종류의 새에요.

Quetzal birds are brightly colored. Some quetzals have tails that are longer than their bodies.

케찰 새는 밝은 색을 띠어요. 몇몇 케찰 새들은 몸보다 긴 꼬리를 갖고 있기도 합니다.

Penguins cannot fly. They use their wings to help them swim underwater.
펭귄은 날지 못해요. 펭귄은 물 속에서 수영을 잘 하기위해 날개를 사용합니다.

Emus can run up to 30 miles (50 kilometers) per hour.
에머스는 시간당 30마일(50킬로미터)를 달릴 수 있습니다.

How Birds Help Earth
새가 지구를 돕는 방법

Birds eat many seeds. These seeds come out in their poop. Bird poop helps the seeds grow into new plants.
새는 씨앗을 많이 먹어요. 씨앗들은 새 똥에서 나옵니다. 새똥은 씨앗들이 새로운 식물로 자랄 수 있게 도와줘요.

20

Some birds help plants make new seeds. They bring pollen from male plants to female plants. The female plants can then make seeds. This is called pollination.

어떤 새들은 식물이 새로운 씨앗을 만들 수 있게 도와줘요. 수그루에서 나온 화분을 암그루로 옮겨 줍니다. 그러면 암그루는 씨앗을 만들 수 있어요. 이것을 수분이라고 합니다.

How Birds Help Other Animals

새가 다른 동물을 돕는 방법

Some birds eat bugs that harm other animals.

어떤 새들은 다른 동물들에게 해로운 벌레들을 먹어요.

22

Oxpeckers sit on the backs of zebras, giraffes, and buffalo. They eat bugs called ticks that eat other animals' blood.

소등쪼기새는 얼룩말, 기린 그리고 버팔로 등 위에 앉아있어요. 동물들 피를 빨아 먹는 진드기를 잡아 먹어줘요.

How Birds Help Humans
새가 사람을 돕는 방법

Veery birds will leave an area if a hurricane is on the way. Hurricanes are strong storms that create strong winds and heavy rain.

개똥지빠귀 새는 허리케인이 오면 떠납니다. 허리케인은 강한 바람과 비를 몰고오는 폭풍이에요.

Scientists study veeries so they know when a bad hurricane is going to hit an area.

과학자들은 개똥지빠귀 새가 언제 허리케인이 올지 알 수 있다고 했어요.

Birds in Danger
멸종위기의 새

Some birds have gone extinct. This means there are no more of them left.
어떤 새들은 멸종했어요. 단 한 마리도 남지 않았다는 말입니다.

The Alagoas foliage-gleaner became extinct in 2018. People destroyed their forests in Brazil.
알라고아서이파리새는 2018년에 멸종했어요. 사람들이 브라질에있는 숲을 파괴했기 때문이죠.

Some birds are endangered. This means they may soon go extinct.
몇몇 새들도 멸종위기입니다. 이 뜻은 곧 멸종 될 수도 있다는 말이죠.

The kakapo is also called the owl parrot. They cannot fly and are an easy meal for other hungry animals.
카카포 새도 올빼미 앵무새로 불리어요. 날지못하기 때문에 쉽게 다른 동물들의 먹이가 돼요.

How To Help Birds
새를 돕는 방법

Many birds get trapped in pieces of garbage. They also try to eat garbage. This can hurt them.
많은 새들이 쓰레기 조각에 걸려요.
그리고 쓰레기를 먹기도 하죠.
이것때문에 다치기도 해요.

Many people are organizing garbage clean-ups in their neighbourhoods. This can help keep birds safe.
많은 사람들이 동네 쓰레기 수거를 잘 정리하기 시작했어요. 이런것도 새들을 지킬 수 있습니다.

Quiz
퀴즈

Test your knowledge of birds by answering the following questions. The questions are based on what you have read in this book. The answers are listed on the bottom of the next page.

다음 질문에 답하고 새에 대한 지식을 테스트해봐요. 질문은 책의 내용에 기초합니다. 정답은 다음 페이지 하단에 있어요.

1 Where do birds sleep?
새들은 어데이서 자나요?

2 What do some male birds do to impress female birds?
몇몇 수컷 새들이 암컷 새들을 유혹하기위해 어떻게 하나요?

3 Why do most female birds sit on their eggs?
암컷 새들은 왜 알 위에 앉나요?

4 What two birds can learn to talk?
어떤 두마리 새가 말하는 법을 배울 수 있나요?

5 What is the most common kind of bird?
제일 흔한 새는 어떤 종류인가요?

6 What do oxpeckers eat?
소등쪼기새는 무엇을 먹나요?

Explore other books in the Animals That Make a Difference series.

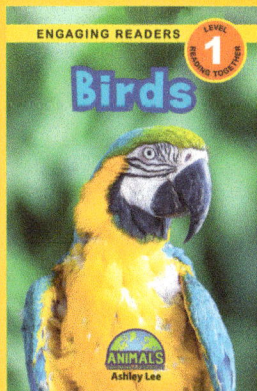

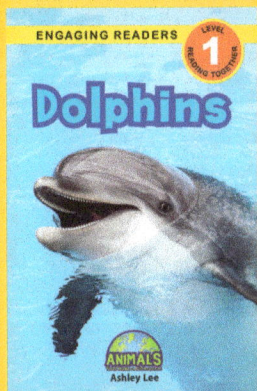

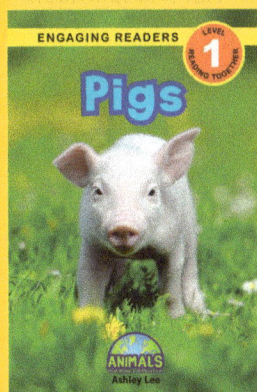

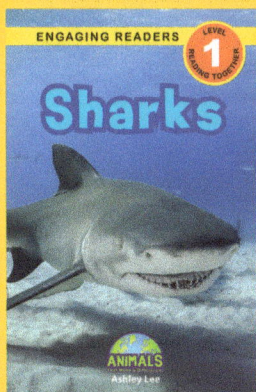

ENGAGING READERS — LEVEL 1 — READING TOGETHER
Bees
ANIMALS
Jared Siemens

ENGAGING READERS — LEVEL 1 — READING TOGETHER
Bats
ANIMALS
Ashley Lee

ENGAGING READERS — LEVEL 1 — READING TOGETHER
Birds
ANIMALS
Ashley Lee

ENGAGING READERS — LEVEL 1 — READING TOGETHER
Dolphins
ANIMALS
Ashley Lee

ENGAGING READERS — LEVEL 1 — READING TOGETHER
Horses
ANIMALS
Ashley Lee

ENGAGING READERS — LEVEL 1 — READING TOGETHER
Ladybugs
ANIMALS
Ashley Lee

ENGAGING READERS — LEVEL 1 — READING TOGETHER
Pigs
ANIMALS
Ashley Lee

ENGAGING READERS — LEVEL 1 — READING TOGETHER
Sharks
ANIMALS
Ashley Lee

ENGAGING READERS — LEVEL 1 — READING TOGETHER
Squirrels
ANIMALS
Ashley Lee

Visit www.engagebooks.com to explore more Engaging Readers.

www.ingramcontent.com/pod-product-compliance
Lightning Source LLC
Chambersburg PA
CBHW051235020426

42331CB00016B/3383